ICT

Finding and Sorting Information

Anne Rooney

QED Publishing

First published in the UK in 2004 by
QED Publishing
A Quarto Group company
226 City Road
London EC1V 2TT

www.qed-publishing.co.uk

Reprinted in 2007

A Catalogue record for this book is available
from the British Library.

ISBN 978 1 84538 874 4

Written by Anne Rooney
Consultant: Philip Stubbs
Designed by Jacqueline Palmer
Editor: Anna Claybourne
Illustrator: John Haslam
Photographer: Ray Moller
Models supplied by Scallywags

Creative Director: Louise Morley
Editorial Manager: Jean Coppendale

Printed and bound in China

The words in **bold**
are explained in the
Glossary on page 31.

Contents

What's it all about?   4

How does it work?   6

Paper or computer?   8

Build your own database   10

Starting your database   12

Making it work   14

Looking up facts   16

The world's biggest database   18

Finding what you want   20

Checking your facts   22

Sharing information   24

Projects to try   26

More projects to try   28

Grown-up zone   30

Glossary   31

Index   32

What's it all about?

Do you know what goes on in your brain? It's a huge information factory. During your life you'll use it to learn lots of facts, make connections between them and store the ones you need to remember.

Un, deux, trois...

Yum yum! Beans for tea.

Tigers love swimming.

Brains and computers

You can store a huge amount of information in your brain – and there's loads you can do with it.

However, no one can remember everything they've ever learned, and we soon forget information we don't use very often. That's where a computer can help.

Full of facts

A computer system for storing, comparing and sorting facts is called a database. A database can be very small, and keep a specific set of facts – such as the heights of all the children in a class. Or it can be very large and store huge amounts of information – such as details of every movie ever made.

Ready to go?

In this book you'll find out how to use databases to store, find and work with information in lots of different ways. You'll make databases of your own to work with information you've gathered, and you'll use the World Wide Web to collect even more facts.

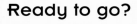

How does it work?

Usually, a database groups together information that's related in some way. For example, it could store information about the members of a club or the things for sale in a shop.

Everyday databases

You could make a database of all your CDs, listing all the artists, all the songs and when each CD was released. Your school has a database of information about all the pupils. It has details like your name, address and date of birth. If you belong to a fan club or library, or subscribe to a magazine, it probably has a database of all its members, too.

GAME ZONE
Customer Club

Sukhjit Misra
2232 362347823 6C 778

There are databases all around us in our everyday lives. If you use an encyclopedia on CD-ROM, that's a database. And if you buy things in a shop and use a loyalty card, the shop's database keeps a record of what you've bought.

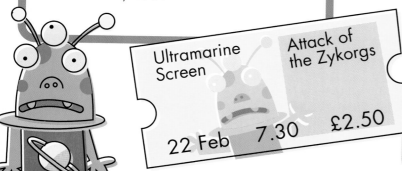

Ultramarine Screen

Attack of the Zykorgs

22 Feb   7.30   £2.50

Fact-finding

Storing lots of information is all very well, but unless you can find the facts you want easily, it's not much use.

Imagine a big book of facts without an index. You know there's lots of information in there, but how are you going to find out what you need to know? Without an index, you'd just have to read through each page in turn. It would take a very long time. Encyclopedias and phone books are arranged in alphabetical order.

Databases, too, need ways to help you to find information. Unlike a book, a database can change the order it shows you information. For example, you could look at a list of kings and queens in alphabetical or chronological order.

Paper or computer?

In all your work, it's worth thinking about whether you really need to use the computer, or whether there might be a better way. For working with facts and figures, a database on the computer is often best.

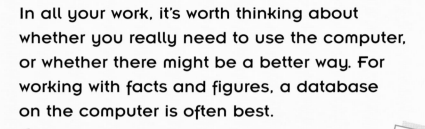

Basketball scores
Ty 'Springer' Daniels   24 goals
Zeb Watson   29 goals
'Tall Paul' McCoy   3 goals
AJ Elliot

Sporting heroes

Imagine you want to keep a list of the top players in a particular sport, and how many goals each has scored. As more matches are played, you add more details.

If you kept your notes on paper, you'd have to decide how to list the players — by team or alphabetically by name. You'd also need to add up the scores for each player. This would change each week, so you'd have to work them out all over again.

This week's results...

If you kept your list on the computer, it could add up all the goals for you, and tell you who had the best score so far every week.

You could use your sports data to make a set of collector's cards — one on each player.

How computers help

Keeping a database on a computer helps in several different ways:

- The computer can automatically compare facts or do calculations for you. On paper, you'd have to look through them all and do the sums yourself.

- You can easily sort information into any order, almost instantly. If you keep a list on paper, it takes some time to re-order your facts.

- You can print out your information any time you add new facts. On paper, you'd have to copy it all out again each time.

- A computer can find information very quickly, but on paper you have to read through the whole lot to find what you want.

Sometimes, though, a paper list may be better. You can carry it around easily with you, use it when you can't get to the computer, and add your own pictures or stickers.

Build your own database

If you have a database program on your computer, you can start making your own databases. You might make a database to help with a hobby or as part of your schoolwork.

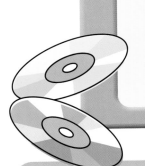

Think first

Before you start making your database, work out what information you want to put in it. You might have the information handy, or you might have to collect facts for your database.

Survey questions

Make sure you ask relevant questions. For example, if you're finding out about cool places, it's not relevant to ask people what their favourite colour is.

Make your questions as useful as possible. Ask for date of birth, not age. Ages change every year, but a database can work out ages from dates of birth.

Doing a survey

One way to get information is to do a survey. You can draw up a list of questions on paper. If there are only a few possible answers to a question, use multiple choice questions with tick boxes for different options.

Date of birth
25 May 1994
– age 10

Date of birth
19 July 1982
– age 22

Date of birth
31 April 1947
– age 57

Question time

Imagine you wanted to make a database of fun things to do in your town. You'd work out the best questions, then make them into a data collection sheet.

Cool things to do in our town

Please fill in details of your favourite place to go.

What is it called? _____

What type of place is it? (tick one)

☐ Sports place
☐ Cinema/theatre
☐ Outdoor place (eg park, zoo)
☐ Café
☐ Other

What can you do there? _____

How much does it cost? (per hour/session) _____

What's the phone number? _____

Does it have a web address? _____

Thank you for taking part

Put it to the test

Next, decide who to include in your survey. Is your database only for young people, or should you ask people of all ages? Then, think about all the answers you might get and see if any of your questions could be better. For example, people might just answer 'yes' to the last question – so you might change it to 'What is the web address?'.

Starting your database

Once you've collected all the information you need, you can make a start on building your database.

Records and fields

A database divides information up into **records** and **fields**.

Each thing for which you have information has its own record. In a database of cars, there'd be one record for each car.

Each fact in a record goes in a space called a field. In your car database, each record might have fields for the make, model and engine size of the car.

If you made a database of horses at a stable, you'd have a record for each horse, with fields for, say, the name, the date of birth (D.O.B), the height and the colour of the horse.

DO IT!

Using your database software, start a new database. The first thing to do is set up the types of fields that will be used in each record and give each field a name, such as 'Date of birth' or 'Phone number'.

You'll need to choose the type of field – for instance, numbers, text or dates.

Name: Tora
D.o.B: 21.12.99
Height: 15 hands
Colour: brown

Putting in your information

You put information into your database by typing in the fields on each record.

You'll need to make a new record for each item you have information about.

TAKE CARE

Check the information is correct before you enter it, and copy it into the computer carefully. The computer can't correct mistakes for you and you'll get the wrong answers out of the database if you put the wrong information in. When you've finished, print everything out and check it.

Cool places

Record → Venue name

Field → Greenhill Sports Centre

Name of field → Venue type

Tick box → ☒ Sports place
☐ Cinema/theatre
☐ Outdoor place (eg park, zoo)
☐ Café
☐ Other

Facilities

Information as text → swimming pool, gymnasium, football pitch, baseball pitch

Cost per hour/session

Information as numbers → £ 5.50

Phone number

01111 22222

Web address

www.greenhillsports.com

Making it work

Once you've put all your information into your database you can make lists, graphs or charts from it.

Putting things in order

You can look at the information in your database in different ways by asking the database to put the records in order for you. This is called **sorting** the database.

For example, you might want your 'Cool places' database to show you a list of places in order of price, with the cheapest first. To do this, you'd need to:

• Choose the field you want to see information about – in this case, it's the 'Cost' field.

• Tell the computer how to sort the information. To see the cheapest prices first, tell the computer to list the entries in order of cost.

DO IT!

In your database program, the option to sort your database will probably be called 'Sort' or 'Reorder'. You should be able to choose ascending order (going up, for example from A–Z or from 1–9) or descending order (going down, from Z–A or from 9–1).

You can print out a list of the information in the order you've chosen.

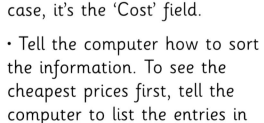

Screen Ultramarine £2.50
Finn's Funfair £3.25
Movieland £3.70
Jedley Zoo £5
Greenhill Sports £5.50

Graphs and charts

Most databases will let you make a graph, using the information stored in them. It's often easier to see facts by looking at a graph than by reading numbers.

Imagine you had a database on people's pets. You could get the database to draw a graph to show how many children in your class had each type of pet.

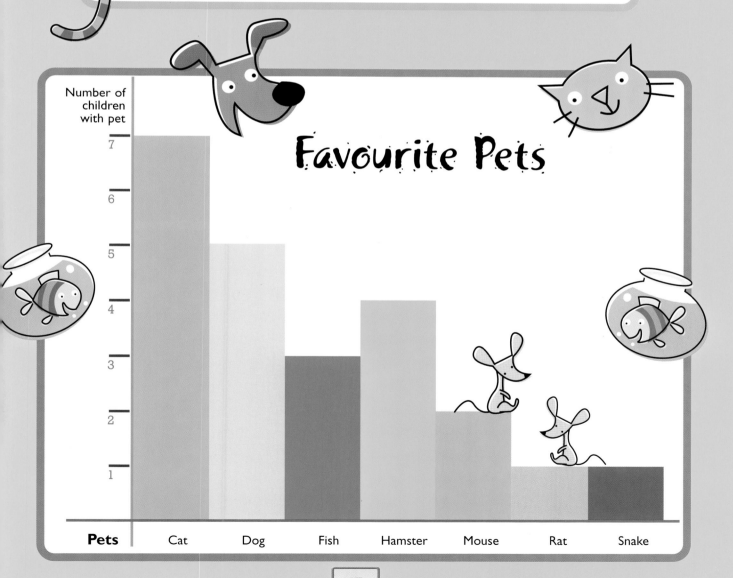

Number of children with pet

7
6
5
4
3
2
1

Pets Cat   Dog   Fish   Hamster   Mouse   Rat   Snake

Favourite Pets

Looking up facts

Sometimes you will want to find particular items in a database. You'll need to tell the database what you're looking for and ask it to find anything that matches.

Ask the database

Suppose you want to use your 'Cool places' database to find all the sports places, or all the cinemas. You find them by asking the database a question called a **query**, or by setting a **filter**.

To do this, you usually have to fill in a form on screen showing what you want to find. The computer will look for things in the fields you fill in. It will ignore any fields you leave blank.

For example, you could look for cinemas like this:

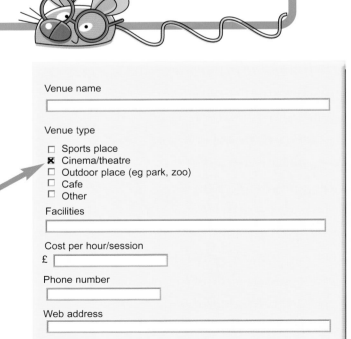

Venue name

Venue type

☐ Sports place
☒ Cinema/theatre
☐ Outdoor place (eg park, zoo)
☐ Cafe
☐ Other

Facilities

Cost per hour/session
£

Phone number

Web address

Finding out more

What if you want to find something more specific – such as all cinemas that cost less than £5?

For things like this, you can use special symbols, called **operators**, to find numbers in a particular range.

This search would find cinemas that cost less than £5.

= means equals
eg **Cost = £5**
means 'find prices that are exactly £5'

> means more than
eg **Cost > £5**
means 'find prices over £5'

< means less than
eg **Cost < £5**
means 'find prices under £5'

Venue name

Venue type

☐ Sports place
✗ Cinema/theatre
☐ Outdoor place (eg park, zoo)
☐ Café
☐ Other

Facilities

Cost per hour/session
£ `<5`

Phone number

Web address

Make it match

In some databases, you search for results by entering a whole phrase, such as **Cost <£5**, into a search box. Make sure you always use the same words the database uses. For example, if a field is named **Cost**, you must use the word **Cost**, not a different word like **price**, because the computer won't recognize it.

Does not compute...!

The world's biggest database

The biggest database in the world is the World Wide Web. Everything you want to know is probably out there somewhere!

Get started on the Web

To use the World Wide Web, you need to make sure your computer is connected to the **Internet**, and start up a **web browser**, such as Internet Explorer or Netscape. Ask for help if you're not sure how to do this.

Starting from home

The page your web browser shows when it starts up is called your home page. You can always get back to it by clicking the Home button in your browser.

Moving around

If you know which web page you want to look at, type in its web address accurately, and then press the Enter or Return key.

Web links

When you get to the page you want, there might be links to other useful information. A link is usually underlined and shown in a different colour, like this: <u>Great white shark</u>.

Going back

If you end up somewhere you don't want to be, or see something you're not comfortable with, click on the Back button to go back a page, or on the Home button to start again.

Back and Forward buttons
Click here to jump back or forward one page.

Home button
Click here to start again.

List of favourite sites (or bookmarks)
Click on the one you want.

Web browser

Website address
Carefully type in the address of the site you want.

Links
Click on these to get to other pages. There are web links in the text, too.

Dropdown menu
A menu like this may appear when you click on a button.

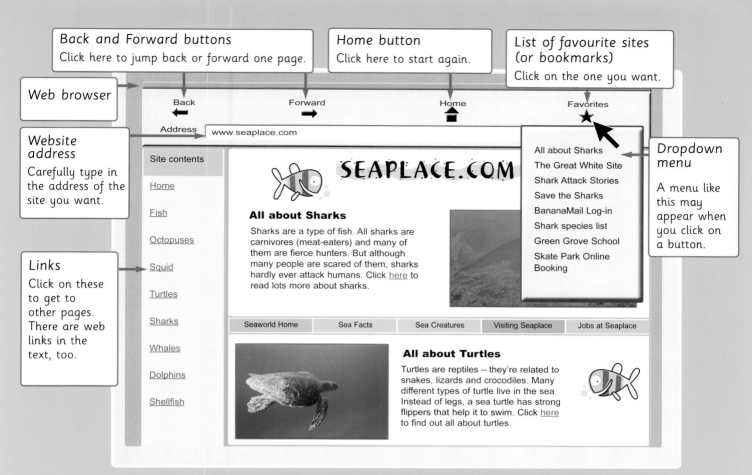

Back   Forward   Home   Favorites ★

Address   www.seaplace.com

All about Sharks
The Great White Site
Shark Attack Stories
Save the Sharks
BananaMail Log-in
Shark species list
Green Grove School
Skate Park Online Booking

Site contents

Home

Fish

Octopuses

Squid

Turtles

Sharks

Whales

Dolphins

Shellfish

SEAPLACE.COM

All about Sharks

Sharks are a type of fish. All sharks are carnivores (meat-eaters) and many of them are fierce hunters. But although many people are scared of them, sharks hardly ever attack humans. Click here to read lots more about sharks.

| Seaworld Home | Sea Facts | Sea Creatures | Visiting Seaplace | Jobs at Seaplace |

All about Turtles

Turtles are reptiles – they're related to snakes, lizards and crocodiles. Many different types of turtle live in the sea. Instead of legs, a sea turtle has strong flippers that help it to swim. Click here to find out all about turtles.

Best places

If you find a web page you like, and you think you might want to use it again, you can add it to a list of your favourite sites. If you're using Internet Explorer, these are called **Favorites**, and if you're using Netscape they're called **Bookmarks**.

'Favorites' is spelled the American way because Internet Explorer is made by an American company!

DO IT!

Open the Bookmarks or Favorites menu in your browser, and click on 'Add' to add the page to your list. Remember what the page is called in the list, so that you can find it again later.

When you want to go back to it again, open the menu. Then click on the name of the page you want to go back to.

Finding what you want

There are two ways of finding what you want on the Web. You can do a search, or you can use a contents list or directory, which lets you choose from different categories of information.

Working with directories

A **directory page** lists categories of information, such as 'news', 'sport', 'schoolwork help' and 'entertainment'. When you click on one, a list for that topic appears for you to choose again. Eventually, you should get to what you want.

A directory is good if you know roughly what you want to find. If you want to read the latest news, or see which movies are just coming out, a directory can help.

DO IT!

Try these directory pages:

www.yahooligans.com
www.kidgrid.com
http://directory.google.com
(click on 'Kids and Teens')

Directory

News
Schoolwork hel
Sport
Shopping
Entertainment

Entertainment

Music   Video
Dance   Latest Movies
Theatre   Skateboard
Book Reviews   Ice Skate
Art   Drama

Latest Movies

Attack of the Zykorgs
The Magic Skateboard
Beowulf

Searching the Web

To find precise information, say a cake recipe, a search is better.

You search the Web using a special kind of web page called a search page or **search engine**.

You'll need to type in the words you're looking for (called **keywords**), and click a button to start the search. The search engine will list pages that contain your keywords.

How to search

To search for a single word, type it and click the button:

| chocolate | **Search** |

To search for a phrase, put it in quotation marks:

| "chocolate brownies" | **Search** |

To search for several words or phrases, just put them all in:

| "chocolate brownies" recipes | **Search** |

or put '**+**' or '**AND**' between them:

| "chocolate brownies" + recipes | **Search** |

DO IT!

Try these search pages:

www.google.com
www.yahoo.com
www.alltheweb.com
www.altavista.com

Choosing the best keywords takes practice. Don't search for "how to make chocolate brownies" because unless a web page has that exact phrase in it, you won't find anything. But don't be too vague, either. If you just put "recipes" you'd find thousands of pages and it would take you ages to track down brownies!

Checking your facts

Whether you've found information from your own database, from a CD-ROM or from the Web, you need to have a good look at it and decide whether it's what you need.

Asking questions

Whatever you're going to do with the information you've found, you'll need to check that it's:

• Accurate • Reliable • Relevant

Make sure you think about all these things before you use the information you've found.

Accuracy

You can probably trust information you get from an encyclopedia or a CD-ROM to be accurate.

If it's from your own database, it will be right as long as you put in the right information and asked the right questions – so check! Think about the answers you'd expect to get, and if they're very different, check your work again.

• Reliable
– do you trust the place you got it from?

• Relevant
– is it suitable for what you want to use it for?

• Accurate
– is it right?

Reliability

If the information is from the Web, is it from a website you can trust? Anyone can put up web pages and no one checks that they're accurate or true.

The information on websites can be biased too. This means that the people who put up the website want you to think in a particular way.

Relevance

You might find some very interesting information, but if it isn't anything to do with the topic you're working on it's not relevant – so leave it out!

I can trust this Encarta CD-ROM.

No

No to pollution

This protest site 'Fight Pollution' may be biased... But 'The SciTech Museum Kid's Page - Pollution' looks good!

That's a cool pic of Dolly the cloned sheep! But I can't really put that in because it's not about pollution...

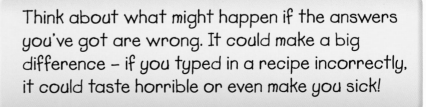

Think about what might happen if the answers you've got are wrong. It could make a big difference – if you typed in a recipe incorrectly, it could taste horrible or even make you sick!

Sharing information

Storing lots of information is only the start. You need to do things with it – like presenting it in a way other people can understand, or printing it out to use later.

Database reports

If you're working with a database of your own, you can print out **reports** which show some or all of the information it stores.

Before printing out your report, you may be able to choose different text styles and arrangements to make it look smarter.

Chocolate recipes

Recipe	Time it takes to make
Chocolate sauce	5 mins
Choc crispies	10 mins
Choco-cherry cookies	15 mins
Choc'n'flake cake	1 hour
Chocolate ice-cream	6 hours

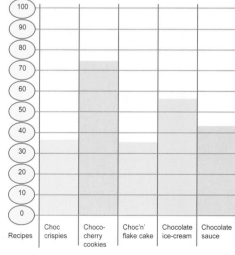

TOP TEN chocolate recipes survey

Votes: 100, 90, 80, 70, 60, 50, 40, 30, 20, 10, 0

Recipes: Choc crispies, Choco-cherry cookies, Choc'n'flake cake, Chocolate ice-cream, Chocolate sauce

Information from the Web

If you're working with information from the Web – or from another large database such as a CD-ROM – you'll need to copy, save or print the information you've found so you can use it for your projects.

You can:

• Print a page out, so you can show it to other people or look at it later.

• Save the page on your computer so that you can look at it without having to connect to the Internet or load the CD.

• Copy words and pictures from a page to put into your own work.

Don't steal!

Words and pictures on the Web are someone else's work, and the law protects other people's work. It's OK to use a bit in something that's just for you, but you can't make lots of copies or include it in a book or a website without getting permission.

 DO IT!

To copy information from the Web, use the mouse to select the words or pictures you want. Choose 'Copy' from the menus at the top of the browser window. Then open a document of your own, and use the 'Paste' option to stick in the bits you've copied.

When you copy something from the Web to use in your own projects, always add a note of the web address where you found it. This will make it easy to check it again later, and will show you're not pretending it's your own work.

Now you know the score, it's time to try it all out for yourself. Here are some suggestions for projects – but, of course, you can change them to make them fit in with your own interests!

Band poster

Use the Web to search for pictures of your favourite band and information about them. Copy some of the stuff you find into a document of your own to make a poster or leaflet about them. You don't have to use the computer to make your poster. Instead, you could print out the words and pictures you find, and cut up the pages so that you can stick the best bits onto a big piece of paper.

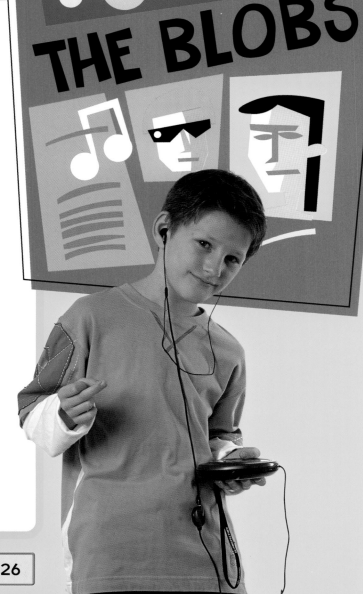

Pet-sitting project

Need to earn some extra pocket money? You could start a pet-sitting service – or just make a database of your friends' pets for fun.

If you really want to look after pets, check with a grown-up first.

Pet database

Make a database for your pet-sitting service. You'll need a record for each pet. Work out what fields you need to put on each record.

It's probably best to list different types of animals and tick the right one on each record. Then you can find all the cats or all the mice with a simple search.

PET SITTING

Animal's name

Animal's age

Owner's name

Owner's phone number

Type of animal:
- [ ] Dog
- [ ] Cat
- [ ] Mouse
- [ ] Hamster
- [ ] Snake

Ask around

Carry out a survey to find out what sorts of pets your friends have. Carefully copy the information into your database. Check the information you've added and try some searches and reports. Could you make the database better? Improve it and try it out again.

Secret spy club

Start a secret spy club with some friends, and keep all your spy details on a secret database. You'll need a record for each member. Work out the fields you'll need for their details.

You could use your database to print out spy ID papers or membership cards for everyone.

Your database program may also let you include pictures, so you can add a photo of each spy and even their fingerprints, copied in with a **scanner**.

TOP SECRET

Agent's name
Jimmy

Password
Claws

Codename
Tiger Eye

Date of birth
16/06/97

Spyphone
0777 441444

Description
150cm tall – short black hair – brown eyes

Special skills
Judo black belt – Skateboard whizz kid

Details of missions
Spying on Shady Street. Inventing new codes.

Codename: Tiger Eye
Date of Birth: 16/06/97
Password: Claws
Spyphone: 0777 441444

Monsters!

Make a database of information about your favourite monsters — they could be dinosaurs, deep-sea fish, monsters from movies or books, or monsters from myths and legends.

Collect all the information you can by searching the Web, and then build a database with a record for each monster. Work out all the different fields you will need on each record.

Here are some ideas for fields.

How big is each monster?

What does it eat?

What does it look like?

Where does it live?

You can also include a field for the addresses of the web pages where you found out about each monster.

Monster File........3

Monster name

| Gorgon |

Monster File........2

Monster name

| Basilisk |

Monster File........1

Monster name

| Cyclops |

Description

| Hideously ugly, with messy hair and one eye in the middle of forehead |

Diet

| Cheese, with occasional raw humans |

Home

| Caves on an island in the Mediterranean Sea |

Info from:

| www.mythsandlegends.com |

Grown-up zone

Fact Factory and the National Curriculum

This book will help a child to cover work units 3C, 4D, 5C and part of 6D of the IT Scheme of Work for the National Curriculum for England and Wales.

The National Curriculum for ICT stresses that ICT should be integrated with other areas of study. This means that a child's use of ICT should fit naturally into other areas of the curriculum. It can be achieved by tasks such as:

- Using a database to record the results of a science experiment or class survey, then presenting or processing the data to show trends or calculate values.

- Using the Web to search for information needed for a topic in literacy or history.

- Using an existing database, such as a CD-ROM, to search for facts needed for a geography report.

Children should incorporate planning, drafting, checking and reviewing their work in all projects. They should discuss with others how their work could be improved, whether ICT methods are the best choice for a given task and how ICT methods compare with manual methods. They should look at ways of combining ICT and manual methods of working.

National Curriculum resources online

ICT programme of study at Key Stage 2 in the National Curriculum:

www.nc.uk.net/nc/contents/ICT-2--POS.html

On teaching ICT in other subject areas:

www.ncaction.org.uk/subjects/ict/inother.htm

ICT schemes of work (you can download a printable copy):

www.standards.dfes.gov.uk/schemes2/it/

The schemes of work for Key Stage 2 suggest ways that ICT can be taught in years 3–6.

Further resources

It's important to make sure that children use the World Wide Web safely. The following sites give advice on how you can protect your children when they work online and how to help them to use the Web sensibly.

www.safekids.com

www.thinkuknow.co.uk

www.yahooligans.com/parents/

www.getnetwise.org

www.nchafc.org.uk/itok/

Glossary

Bookmark

Saved reference to a web page you want to use again.

Directory page

Web page that lists different topics to help you find a particular subject.

Favorite

Saved reference to a web page you want to use again.

Field

Space on a database record for a single item of information about something.

Filter

Way of finding records in a database that match specific requirements.

Internet

Network of computers connected together around the world so that they can share information.

Keyword

Word used to search the World Wide Web or another database.

Operator

Special word or symbol used to help you find information in a database.

Query

Question that you ask of a database in order to find information.

Record

All the information about one particular item in a database.

Report

Printout or screen display of information found in a database.

Scanner

Device for copying pictures from paper into the computer.

Search engine

Web page used to search the World Wide Web.

Sort

Put information from a database into a particular order.

Web browser

Computer program for looking at and moving between web pages.

Index

accuracy 22

back button 18
bookmarks 19, 31
brain 4
browser 18, 31

calculations 9
CD-ROMs 6, 25
charts 15
checking facts 22–3
comparing facts 9
computers 4–5
copying 25

databases 5
    building 10-11
    how they work 6
    searching for facts in
    16–17
    starting 12–13
directories 20
directory pages 20, 31
dropdown menu 19

encyclopedias 6, 7

fact-finding 7, 9, 16–17
    on Web 20–1
favorites 19, 31
fields 12–13, 31
filter 16, 31

finding information
    7, 9, 10–11, 16–17
    in database 16–17
    on Web 20–1

graphs 15

home button 18, 19
home page 18, 19

index 7
Internet 18, 31
Internet Explorer 18, 19

keywords 21, 31

law 25
libraries 7
links 18, 19
lists 8–9
loyalty cards 6

monster database project
    29

Netscape 18, 19

operators 17, 31

paper lists 8, 9
pasting 25
pet database project 27
photographs 28

pictures 25, 28
poster project 26
printing out 9, 14, 24, 25
programs 14
projects 26–9

queries 16, 31

records 12–13
relevance 22, 23
reliability 22, 23
reordering information 14
reports 24, 31

saving pages 25
scanner 31
search engine 21, 31
searching:
    database 16–17
    the Web 21
secret spy club project 28
sharing information 24–5
sorting 9, 14, 31
stealing 25
storing information 4–5
surveys 10–11, 27
symbols 17

typing information 13

web address 18, 19
web browser 18, 31
World Wide Web
    5, 18–21, 25